# Two's Company...

by Shirley Greenway

Photographs by Oxford Scientific Films

Charlesbridge

Conceived, designed, and produced by
White Cottage Children's Books
29 Lancaster Park
Richmond, Surrey TW10 6AB, England

First published 1997 in the United States of America
by Charlesbridge Publishing
85 Main Street, Watertown, MA 02172-4411
(617) 926-0329

**Library of Congress Cataloging-in-Publication Data**
Greenway, Shirley
        Two's company—/ by Shirley Greenway; photographs by
Oxford Scientific Films.
        p.    cm.
        Summary: From a gaggle of geese to a pride of lions, the
names for groups of animals are introduced in brief text and
photographs.
        ISBN 0-88106-963-9 (reinforced for library use)
        ISBN 0-88106-962-0 (softcover)
        1. Animals—Juvenile literature. 2. English language—
collective nouns—juvenile literature. (1. English language—
Collective nouns.
2. English language—Terms and phrases. 3. Animals.)
1. Oxford Scientific Films. II. Title.
QL49.G754 1997
428.1—dc20                                                          96-23968

Printed in Singapore
(hc) 10 9 8 7 6 5 4 3 2 1
(sc) 10 9 8 7 6 5 4 3 2 1

To Mattachin and Hiroshige —
two's company...

—S. G.

Photographer credits: *Title page*—Steve Turner;
*Introduction*—Rudie Kuiter; *Sheep*—John
Downer (above left), Hans Reinhard/Okapia
(below left and right); *Fish*—Tom McHugh/Photo
Researchers; *Fox*—Konrad Wothe (above left),
Daniel J. Cox (below left), G.A. Maclean (right);
*Bee*—David Thompson (left), Phil Devries (right);
*Sunflower*—Alain Christof; *Zebra*—Bruce
Davidson (left), Anthony Bannister (right); *Snow
goose*—John Gerlach/Animals Animals (above
left), Michael W. Richards (below left), Miriam
Austerman (right); *Dolphin*—Howard Hall;
*Macaw*—Daniel J. Cox (above left), Frank
Schneidermeyer (below left), Michael Fogden
(right); *Kangaroo*—Hans & Judy Beste (above
left), Des & Jen Bartlett/Survival (below left),
Kathie Atkinson (right); *Harvest mouse*—G.I.
Bernard; *Camel*—Mickey Gibson/Animals
Animals (left), David Shale/Survival (right);
*Walrus*—William Bacon/Photo Researchers
(above left), Jeff Lepore/Photo Researchers
(below left), Lon Lauker (right); *Lion*—Steve
Turner (above left), William Paton/Survival
(below left), Des & Jen Bartlett/Survival (right);
*Tailpiece*—Dr. A.C. Twomey/Photo Researchers.

---

The text type and display type were set in Brooklyn and Bodnoff by R & B Creative Services.

Color separations were made by Bright Arts HK Limited, Hong Kong.

Printed and bound by Imago Publishing Limited

Edited by Treld Pelkey Bicknell

Designed by Glynn Pickerill

---

Some animals live alone,
some live in families,
and some live in groups,
each with its own special name.
   Two is company, but three
can be a flock or a herd,
a school or a pod . . .

**O**ne sheep alone,

**two** sheep together–

a **flock** of sheep
grazing in the snow.

**O**ne small fish,

**two** shimmering
fish –

a **shoal** of
silvery fish swimming.

**O**ne fox sniffing,

**two** foxes digging–

a **skulk** of foxes

hunting in the night.

**O**ne honeybee working,

**two** honeybees
around a flower–

a **swarm** of honeybees buzzing.

**O**ne zebra on the savanna,

**two** friendly zebras in the bush—

a **herd** of zebras
gathered at the watering hole.

**O**ne goose floating,

**two** geese flying–

a **gaggle** of geese
rising into the sky.

**O**ne dolphin somersaulting in the sea,

**two** dolphins swimming together–

a **school** of dolphins gliding
through blue water.

**O**ne macaw
all alone,

**two** macaws
meeting–

a **family** of macaws
sitting on a wall.

**O**ne kangaroo hopping,

**two** kangaroos boxing–

a **troop** of kangaroos resting in the shade.

**O**ne mouse nibbling,

**two** mice kissing–

a **nest** of mice

hidden in the grass.

# One stately camel,

**two** comical camels–

a **train** of camels traveling
across the sand.

**O**ne walrus
showing his
fine tusks,

**two** walruses enjoying a swim –

a **pod** of walruses sunbathing
on the rocks

**O**ne lazy lion yawning,

**two** contente___s resting–

a **pride** of lions drinking in the afternoon.

So, whether you
belong to a family or a pair,
a group or a gathering,
a class or a crowd –
it's nice to be one,
and fun to be two,
but sometimes it's good to be many!

# ...and another thing!

The familiar grazing **Sheep** *(Ovis aries)* is a descendant of the wild mouflon. The earliest of all domesticated animals, sheep have been bred for wool, milk, and meat for about twelve thousand years. There are now more than four hundred different breeds worldwide.

The hard-working **Honeybee** *(Apis mellifera)* can be found wherever flowers grow. It collects nectar and pollen for honey-making in special sacs in its abdomen and on its legs. When a honeybee finds a rich nectar source, she will "dance" its exact location on the surface of the honeycomb to guide the other workers.

The **Threadfin Shad** *(Dorosoma petenense)* is a round-bodied relative of the herring. This silvery-blue fish can be found in vast shoals in the warmer waters of North America and Asia, where they feed on plankton.

There are three types of zebras. The most common is **Burchell's Zebra** *(Equus burchelli)* which lives on the plains of Africa. The striking pattern of black and white stripes is unique to each individual—helping members of the herd recognize and signal another.

The **Red Fox** *(Vulpes vulpes fulva)* is nocturnal. At dusk it leaves its den to hunt, using its sharp senses of sight and hearing. The fox has been hunted for thousands of years. It survives—and thrives—by being both clever and adaptable.

The **Lesser Snow Goose** *(Anser caerulescens)* breeds on Arctic islands. Its migration flight takes it to the shores and estuaries of North America for the summer. The black-tipped ends of its pure white feathers can be seen as the snow goose opens its wings in flight—becoming part of a perfect arrow of elegant white birds against the sky.

The **Dolphin** *(Delphinus delphis)* is found in all the world's oceans. A sleek-skinned and graceful sea mammal, it is fun-loving and intelligent—with great navigational skills and a complex "language" of clicks and whistles.

The lofty **Arabian Camel** *(Camelus dromedarius)*, with its long legs, tough padded feet, and store of fat in its single hump, is well suited to life in the desert. It can exist for several weeks with little food or water. The camel has been valued by desert people for its strength and endurance for thousands of years.

The **Scarlet Macaw** *(Ara chloroptera)* is one of the most beautiful members of the parrot family, with its glossy, brightly colored feathers. Macaws screech through the tropical forests of Central and South America, feeding on fruits and hard-shelled nuts, which they crack with their strong beaks.

The **Walrus** *(Odobenus rosmarus)* lives in Arctic waters, protected from the icy cold by its thick skin and layers of insulating blubber. Using its long, strong tusks, the walrus "hauls out" on dry land to sunbathe until its wrinkled skin grows pink.

The **Great Gray Kangaroo** *(Macropus giganteus)*, which lives in the open forests of Australia, is the world's largest marsupial. A marsupial is an animal with a pouch in which the mother carries her young. Kangaroos use their huge tails for balance as they bound through the grass on their strong hind legs.

The **Lion** *(Panthera leo)*, with its large, maned head, steady gaze, and tawny coat, is the most impressive of the big cats. But the smaller lioness is the more fearsome hunter—able to bring down a running antelope or a small elephant with a swift burst of speed. Humans are the lion's only natural enemies.

The **Harvest Mouse** *(Micromys minutus)* is one of the world's smallest mammals. It is so tiny that it can scamper along a stalk of wheat without bending it. Harvest mice use their extra-long tails as anchors, leaving their front paws free to gather nuts and berries.